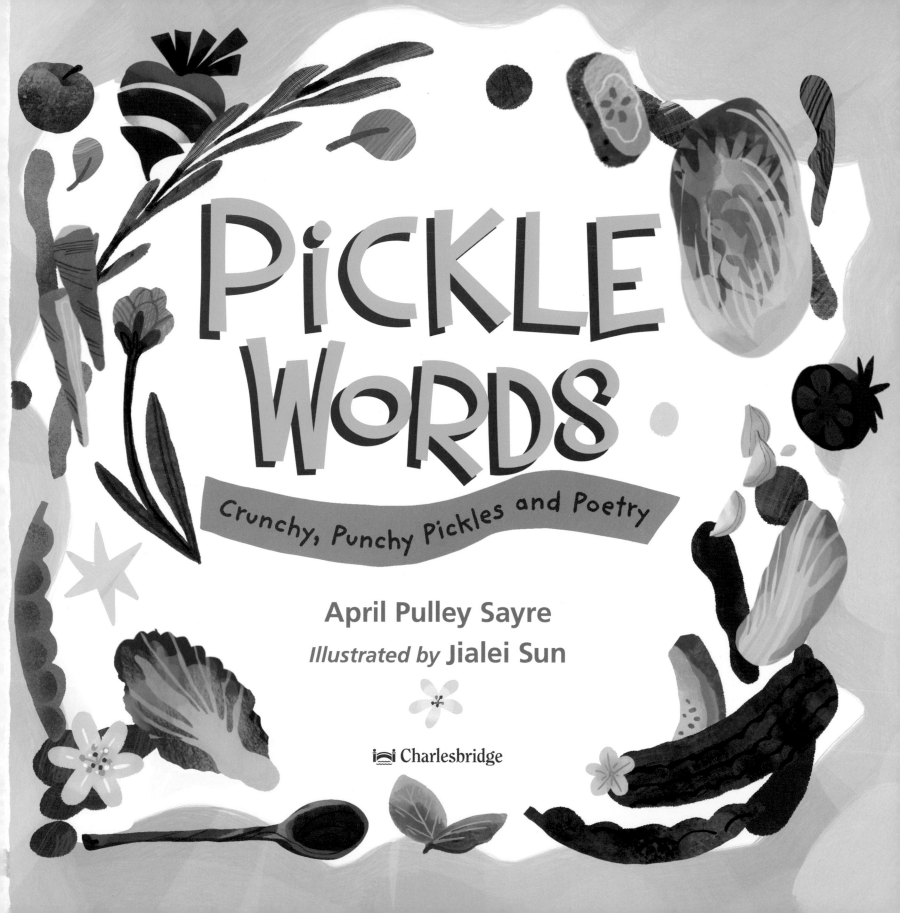

PICKLE WORDS

Crunchy, Punchy Pickles and Poetry

April Pulley Sayre

Illustrated by **Jialei Sun**

ini **Charlesbridge**

For Abby, Madeline, Ellen, and Derek.
For Violet, Heather, and Nate.—A. P. S.

To my dearest mother and grandparents
for the love and hometown flavors you shared.—J. S.

Special thanks to Judith Sumner, botanist, pickling expert, and author of *American Household Botany, The Natural History of Medicinal Plants,* and *Plants Go to War,* for sharing her invaluable advice and expertise.

Published by Charlesbridge
9 Galen Street, Watertown, MA 02472
(617) 926-0329 • www.charlesbridge.com

Library of Congress Cataloging-in-Publication Data
Names: Sayre, April Pulley, author. | Sun, Jialei, illustrator.
Title: Pickle words / April Pulley Sayre; illustrated by Jialei Sun.
Description: Watertown, MA: Charlesbridge, 2024. | Includes bibliographical references. | Audience: Ages 4–8 | Audience: Grades 2–3 | Summary: "Rhyming poetry celebrates the pickling process and all things pickled, including cucumbers, cabbage, peppers, and more. The art tells the story of a diverse neighborhood that comes together to share family recipes and pickle poetry. Back matter includes a recipe, scientific information, and a visual glossary of pickles from around the world."—Provided by publisher.
Identifiers: LCCN 2022013973 (print) | LCCN 2022013974 (ebook) | ISBN 9781623543624 (hardcover) | ISBN 9781632893338 (ebook)
Subjects: LCSH: Pickled foods. | Canning and preserving. | LCGFT: Cookbooks.
Classification: LCC TX805 .S29 2024 (print) | LCC TX805 (ebook) | DDC 641.4/62—dc23/eng/20220322
LC record available at https://lccn.loc.gov/2022013973
LC ebook record available at https://lccn.loc.gov/2022013974

Printed in China
(hc) 10 9 8 7 6 5 4 3 2 1

Illustrations done in digital media
Display type set in Mister Sirloin BTN Medium by Stuart Sandler
Text type set in Andes by Daniel Hernandez
Printed by 1010 Printing International Limited in Huizhou, Guangdong, China
Production supervision by Jennifer Most Delaney
Designed by Cathleen Schaad

Peter Piper
picked a peck.
Can you speak in pickles?
Check!

Summer produce
by the pile?
Pickle it!
Make it last a while.

bumpy

colorful

smelly

fresh

juicy

Pickling is a way of preserving food in vinegar, salted water, or a mixture of the two.

Clean. Sort. Soak.
Straight. Curved. Bent.

Wait, wait, wait
till they ferment!

spears

slices

Pickle making starts with washing and sorting fruits and vegetables. Fresh, blemish-free cucumbers that fit in canning jars can become whole pickles. But sometimes it's hard not to eat them right away!

Quick pickles, or refrigerator pickles, are made in a few minutes or hours. The vegetables are soaked in brine—a mixture of water, salt, and vinegar. Flavorings such as dill, garlic, or mustard seed are added.

salty

Pickle packers,
dill and fill!
Pour the brine.
Seal or chill!

Sauerkraut

long-lasting

tart

snappy

Fermented pickles take weeks
or even months to make. Picklers pack
vegetables in a salty brine, seal the jar, and
wait. Sealing the jar keeps air out, allowing
anaerobic bacteria—which thrive without
air—to change the vegetables' texture and
develop their pickle flavor.

Clean the cabbage.
Coat with paste.
Onions. Garlic.
Sauce to taste!

spicy

Kimchi is a Korean dish of salted and fermented vegetables. One of the most popular types of kimchi is made from napa cabbage that has been rubbed with spicy red-pepper paste.

김치

Cross sections. Quarters.
Whole with stem.

bright

Some pickle makers use whole fruits and vegetables. Others pare and chop their produce to make chutney or relish.

Chunks for chutney!
Relish them!

Gherkins workin'.
Mustard—wow!
Piccalilli.
Chowchow now!

Piccalilli and chowchow are relishes made of chopped-up vegetables such as gherkins (a type of cucumber), cabbage, bell peppers, green tomatoes, and cauliflower, and spices such as mustard powder, turmeric, and ginger.

tasty

Chowchow

Craving cabbage?
Kimchi's out?
Check the crock for
sauerkraut.

Like kimchi, sauerkraut is cabbage that has been fermented in salt with spices. Common sauerkraut spices include caraway seeds, dill seeds, celery seeds, and juniper berries.

flavorful

punchy

Icy slices.
Crisp, red, green.
Pepper rings
for in between.

versatile

Pickles are usually side dishes or condiments—not the main dish, but something that heightens the flavor of foods. You can stack pickle slices in sandwiches or on pizza, squirt relish on a hot dog, or crunch on cubes of pickled Korean radish with your bibimbap.

Family recipes!
Dice. Spice. Chili.

Pull a pickle face—
sour or silly!

funny

puckery

Pickles, with their sharp, spicy tastes, are memorable. No wonder family recipes are passed down through generations. Humans have been making pickles for at least four thousand years.

Rubbery. Wrinkled.
Lemon and lime.
Squeaky. Leaky.
They're all sublime.

FIRST ANNUAL PICKLE

delicious

diverse

PARTY!

Pickles come in all sorts of shapes, colors, and textures. Around the world, people pickle fruits, vegetables, mushrooms, fish, eggs, flowers, and more.

Snag a spear.
No time to waste.
Pickles and words?
They're worth a taste!

WORLD OF PICKLES

Pennsylvania Dutch red beet eggs:
Pickled eggs from the United States

Suan cai:
Pickled mustard greens from China

Cornichons:
Pickled gherkins from France

Giardiniera:
Pickled vegetables from Italy

Atchar:
Pickled mangoes from South Africa

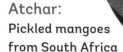

Aceituna Aloreña:
Pickled olives from Spain

Kabees el lift:
Pickled turnips from Lebanon

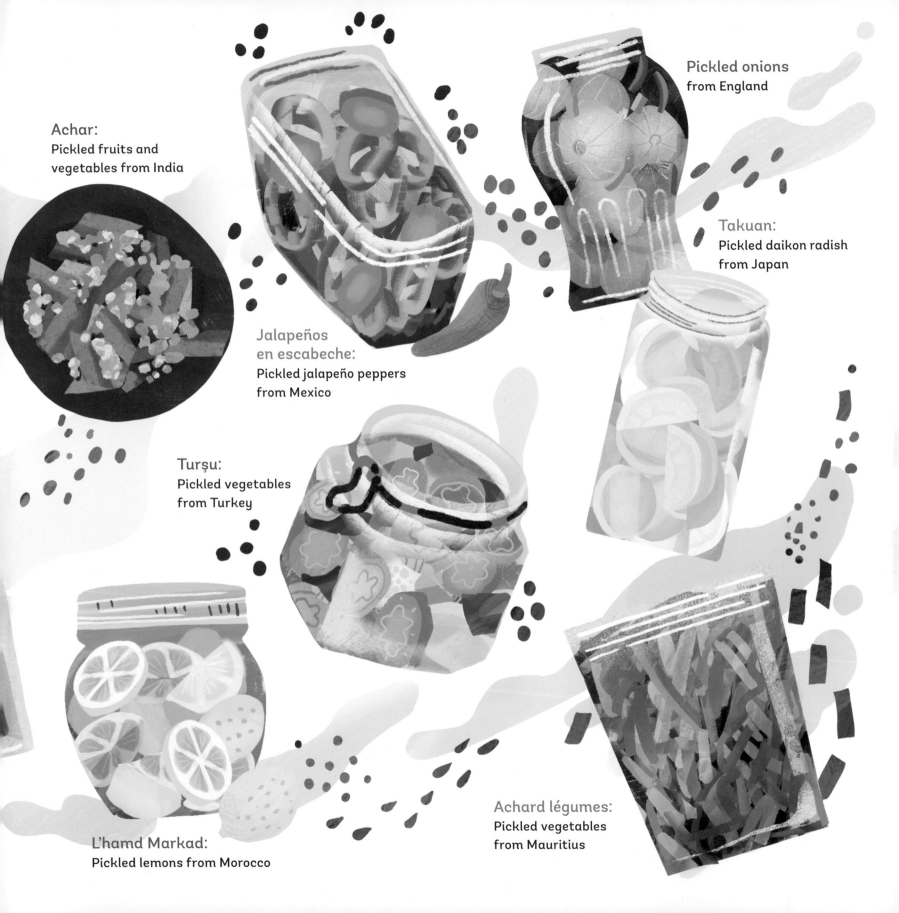

Achar:
Pickled fruits and
vegetables from India

Jalapeños
en escabeche:
Pickled jalapeño peppers
from Mexico

Pickled onions
from England

Takuan:
Pickled daikon radish
from Japan

Turşu:
Pickled vegetables
from Turkey

Achard légumes:
Pickled vegetables
from Mauritius

L'hamd Markad:
Pickled lemons from Morocco

Pick Your Pickling Process!

Pickling is the process of preserving food—usually vegetables and fruit—in an acidic environment. There are three basic types of pickling: fermenting, canning, and quick pickling.

Making Fermented Pickles

Pickle makers first wash the vegetables to remove any yeast or mold. They may cut up the vegetables or leave them whole.

They next mix salt and water (and sometimes vinegar) to make a brine. Herbs and spices can add flavor and help preserve the vegetables.

Pickle makers then pack the vegetables into a jar and pour in the hot brine, making sure to completely submerge the vegetables.

After tightly sealing the jar, it's time to wait! Within the brine, helpful anaerobic bacteria turn the sugar in the vegetables into lactic acid. The acid prevents the growth of harmful bacteria and gives the pickles their sour taste. The longer the pickles ferment, the more tart they'll get.

WARNING: If fermented pickles are exposed to air and kept at room temperature, they can grow harmful molds and bacteria. To avoid food-related illness, pickle makers should carefully follow a tested recipe and refrigerate the pickles after opening. Pickles should not be eaten if there is any mold growth in the jar.

Making Canned Pickles

Canners pack vegetables into a jar and pour in brine. They then loosely screw on the lid and heat the jar in boiling water. This sterilizes the food, killing any bacteria or molds, and forces out the air, creating a tight seal. Sterilizing the pickles preserves them without fermentation.

PICKLED BEETS
5/7/24

Making Quick Pickles

Quick pickles, also called refrigerator pickles, are easier and quicker to make than fermented or canned pickles. Pickle makers pack vegetables into a jar and pour in vinegar (or sometimes citrus juice) and seasoning. The acid in the vinegar preserves the vegetables without fermentation. Quick pickles need to be stored in the fridge and eaten within a few weeks.

Try making quick pickles using the simple recipe on the next page. As with any food preparation, ask an adult for help.

A Few More Bites for Hungry Minds

Books

From Garden to Pickle by Penelope S. Nelson (Jump!, 2021)
Simple text and photographs offer a step-by-step explanation of where pickles come from.

Mrs. Fickle's Pickles by Lori Ries (Boyds Mills, 2006)
In this rhyming story, Mrs. Fickle grows cucumbers from seed and makes pickles from scratch for the county fair.

No Kimchi for Me! by Aram Kim (Holiday House, 2017)
Yoomi is determined to learn to like kimchi so her brothers will stop calling her a baby.

Pickle Party! by Frank Berrios (Random House, 2021)
Two friends learn how to make pickles in this early reader.

Pickles, Please! by Andy Myer (Running Press Kids, 2011)
No one else understands young Alec Smart's passion for pickles—until he visits a pickle factory and meets someone who thinks pickles are just as "picklicious" as he does.

Websites

History in a Jar: The Story of Pickles: www.pbs.org/food/the-history-kitchen/history-pickles/

13 Types of Pickles You Should Know (and Try!): www.tasteofhome.com/collection/types-of-pickles/

Fascinating Pickle Facts: www.exploratorium.edu/cooking/pickles/history.html

Quick Dill Pickles

INGREDIENTS

Pickling cucumbers to fill a large glass jar

5 garlic cloves, sliced

1 head of dill

1 cup cider vinegar

1 quart cold water

6 tablespoons pickling salt

DIRECTIONS

1. Wash the cucumbers.

2. Put half of the garlic and some of the dill into the jar.

3. Pack the cucumbers into the jar.

4. Combine the vinegar, water, and salt to make a brine. Heat to a simmer.

5. Pour the hot brine over the cucumbers in the jar.

6. Add the remaining garlic and dill.

7. Cover the jar and allow it to cool.

8. Refrigerate.

Try a pickle in five days. If you want a stronger flavor, wait another five days.
If you eat up all your pickles, add more cucumbers to the brine!

Delicious Words and Chewy Questions

I love delicious words—words such as *zigzag*, *tetrahedral*, *crepuscular*, *chrysanthemum*, and *squish*. These kinds of words feel good in your mouth. When you read them out loud, they crackle, clank, and bounce in the air.

I also love pickles. When my sisters and I were young, we helped our grandmother scrub cucumbers and make her famous fermented dill pickles, complete with garlic and grape leaves gathered from the garden. Jars of dill pickles and Christmas pickles lined the shelves in the mudroom where we cleaned our muddy hands and boots.

Delicious words and pickles melded by accident when I was grown up and doing author school visits. One day I described a bumpy, barnacle-faced whale in my slideshow as looking like a pickle. The students laughed and nodded. So, as we moved on to discuss word choice, I asked them to brainstorm words related to pickles.

At first the kids came up with straightforward pickle words: *sour*, *salty*, *green*. Soon we advanced to *yellow*, *bumpy*, *lumpy*, *fresh*, *fermented*, *squishy*, *crisp*. Pickles sparked intense memories and opinions in the students. Teachers told me later that many kids who normally didn't speak up had contributed that day. Eventually I shared this "Pickle Words" brainstorming activity with thousands of kids.

What is it about pickles? Perhaps it's the power of sour or the intensity of biting into a food that can surprise you with sweetness, saltiness, crunch, or even a squirt. Maybe it's the magic of the pickling process, which changes taste, color, composition, and form. It is culinary, chemical metamorphosis. And like science experiments—and writing—it can take an unexpected turn, need a little more time, or go a bit wonky, which only adds to the feeling of accomplishment when it works.

This book is for all those students and teachers who shared their delicious words and traditions with me. You helped make my journey a joy.

—April Pulley Sayre, April 2021